AGAINST THE ELEMENTS

FIRE

NIGEL RITCHIE

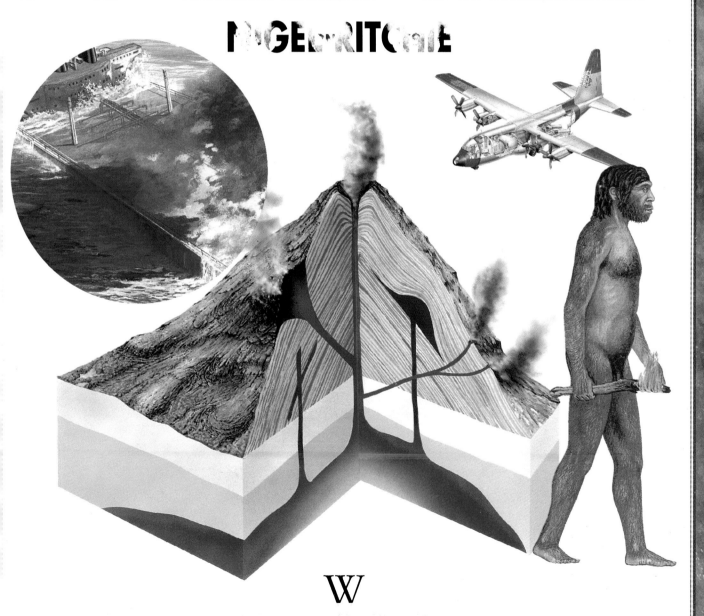

W

This edition published in 2000
© Aladdin Books Ltd 1998

Designed and produced by
Aladdin Books Limited
28 Percy Street
London W1P 0LD

ISBN 0 7496 2786 7 (hardback)
ISBN 0 7496 3887 7 (paperback)

First published in Great Britain in 1998 by
Franklin Watts
96 Leonard Street
London EC2A 4XD

Printed in Belgium

Editor
Simon Beecroft

Design
David West
CHILDREN'S BOOK DESIGN

Designer
Flick Killerby

Illustrators
Mike Saunders, Ian Thompson,
Aziz Khan and Alex Pang

Picture Research
Brooks Krikler Research

Original concept by
Wilgress B. Pipe

A CIP catalogue entry for this book is available
from the British Library.

The author, **Nigel Ritchie**, graduated in
anthropology, and is a freelance writer and
editor of children's books.

The consultant, **David Pedgley**, is a Vice President
of the Royal Meteorological Society, London.

*The author would like to dedicate
this book to Oliver.*

CONTENTS

Introduction

"Fighting fires stretches you to the limit, but some fires are too hot to handle." *Fire-fighter, London, 1997*

Fire is an elemental force that has been both worshipped and feared since time began. It is the result of a chemical reaction between oxygen in the air and flammable material, 'fuel', and is the most common cause of disaster.

Fire can spread at frightening speed and often seems to have a will of its own. A carelessly dropped match can turn a room into a blazing inferno in three minutes, while a heavy wind can transform a small blaze into a major disaster, destroying a whole city in its wake. It is not only people that start fires. Lightning strikes regularly start blazes, while the most awesome sight of fire in action is that of a volcano erupting with a mix of fire, gas and molten lava.

Fighting fires stretches human ingenuity to the limit. Using a wide range of machines – fire engines, water bombers, chemicals and even explosives – fire-fighters go where few dare, risking their lives in perilous conditions. Yet, experience tells us that some fires are bigger than anything we have invented to put them out...

Fire was discovered by early humans.

RITUAL FIRE

The worship of fire is one of the earliest forms of religion and occupies a central position in the religious rites of Hinduism and other Eastern beliefs. It is Hindu tradition in some parts of the world to burn their dead on funeral pyres as an act of purification (right). *Afterwards, the cremated remains are scattered in a sacred river, such as the Ganges.*

In Christianity, candles are burned during many celebrations including Easter (left). *The flame symbolises Jesus, who is described as 'the Light of the World', and his return to life on Easter Sunday.*

FIRE MYTHOLOGY

In mythology, dragons are fire-breathing beasts that may be either ferocious or friendly. European dragons are usually evil beasts (right) that are fought by heroes, whereas Asian dragons more often signify good luck and health.

The ancient people of Easter Island, a remote island in the South Pacific Ocean, used rock from an extinct volcano to create huge carved statues (left). No one is quite sure how they achieved such amazing feats of engineering, since some of the heads stand 12 m (40 ft) tall, and there are over 600 of them on the island. These statues are thought to represent the islanders' mythological ancestors.

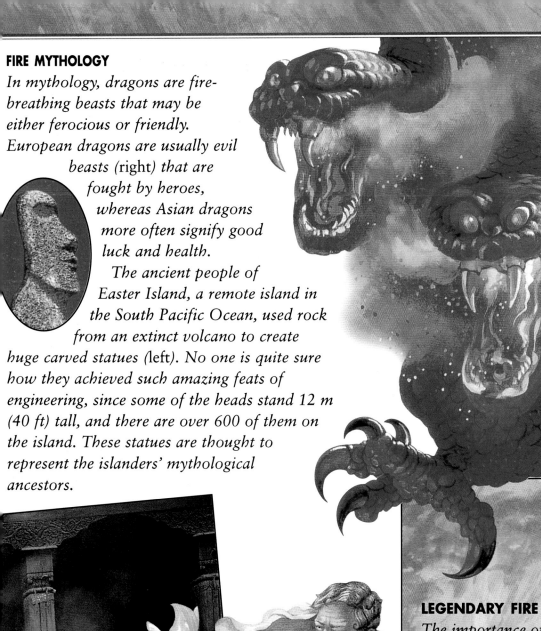

A burning funeral pyre in Kathmandu, Nepal.

LEGENDARY FIRE

The importance of fire is shown by the fact that almost every culture has its own myth of how fire was discovered. In ancient Greek legend, Prometheus (left) was caught stealing back the secret of fire from the gods on Mount Olympus. As punishment, he was chained to a rock and vultures were sent to peck out his liver. But every night it grew back again by magic, so that the torture could be repeated. The Greeks thought that there was a separate god for good and bad fire: Hestia was the good goddess of the hearth and Hephaestus was the god of volcanoes and fiery destruction.

Underwater volcanoes

"The sea began to boil and we saw clouds of smoke." *Crew member describing the birth of the volcanic island of Surtsey, 1963*

On 14 November, 1963, Captain Gudnar Tomasson's boat was trawling for cod in the icy waters of the North Atlantic, when he and his crew were nearly thrown overboard by a large wave. Recovering their balance, they noticed the sea starting to 'boil', and saw huge clouds of smoke rising in the distance. Thinking it was another boat in distress, Tomasson went to investigate, but he soon realised that a volcanic eruption was underway. Fearing for his crew's safety, he sailed away through the clouds of steam and ash, narrowly avoiding the chunks of cooled lava being hurled through the air by periodic explosions. A day later, a new island began to appear above the water, 30 km (20 miles) off the southwest coast of Iceland. This island was named Surtsey, after the Viking fire god, Surt.

Surtsey was formed by lava breaking through a crack in the ocean floor. Chains of volcanic islands, such as Hawaii (*left*), are the tips of volcanoes which form over an area known as a 'hotspot'. Here, lava from a crack in the Earth's crust forms a volcano. The ocean floor is continually shifting so, in time, the volcano moves away from the crack and another forms in its place.

BLACK VOLCANOES

In 1977, the remotely-operated deep-sea submersible, Alvin, was prowling around the freezing depths of the Pacific Ocean, 4,000 m (13,000 ft) below the water surface. Suddenly, temperatures of up to 300°C (600°F) were registered, and bizarre-looking pillars were seen (left). In fact, a whole new community of life was discovered. The pillars, named black smokers, lie near volcanic activity below the sea bed. As super-hot water is forced upwards, the minerals dissolved in it cool and gradually build up to form these black pillars. Weird tube worms with red tips, crabs and sea spiders live around them.

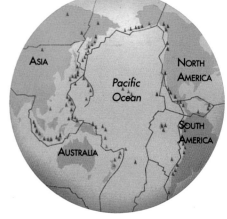

The 'Ring of Fire' is shown by the red areas.

RING OF FIRE

More than three quarters of the world's volcanoes and earthquakes occur in a belt around the Pacific Ocean, known as the 'Ring of Fire'. They occur where magma (red-hot, melted rock) bursts through cracks in the Earth's crust.

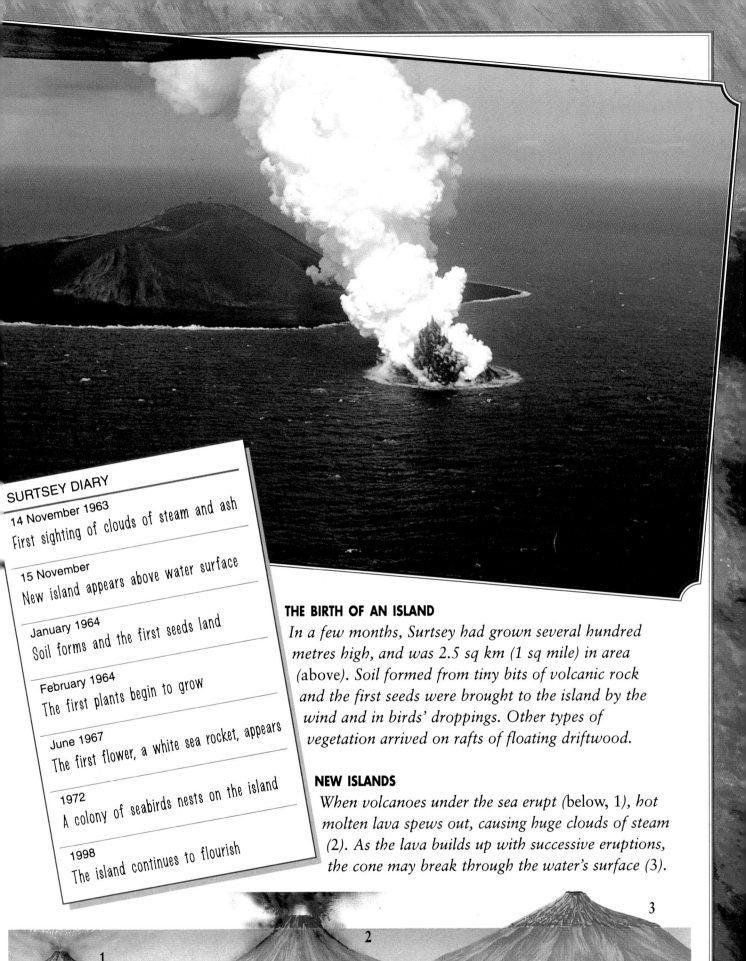

SURTSEY DIARY

14 November 1963
First sighting of clouds of steam and ash

15 November
New island appears above water surface

January 1964
Soil forms and the first seeds land

February 1964
The first plants begin to grow

June 1967
The first flower, a white sea rocket, appears

1972
A colony of seabirds nests on the island

1998
The island continues to flourish

THE BIRTH OF AN ISLAND

In a few months, Surtsey had grown several hundred metres high, and was 2.5 sq km (1 sq mile) in area (above). Soil formed from tiny bits of volcanic rock and the first seeds were brought to the island by the wind and in birds' droppings. Other types of vegetation arrived on rafts of floating driftwood.

NEW ISLANDS

When volcanoes under the sea erupt (below, 1), hot molten lava spews out, causing huge clouds of steam (2). As the lava builds up with successive eruptions, the cone may break through the water's surface (3).

1   2   3

Underwater volcanoes form islands when they erupt.

THE HORROR OF TAMBORA

The weather changes caused by Tambora's eruption in 1815 inspired one of the great modern horror stories! Writers Percy and Mary Shelley and Lord Byron were staying at Lake Geneva, when the weather became oddly cold and dark for the time of year. Forced to stay indoors, they told ghost stories to suit the eerie mood and this inspired Mary Shelley to write her book Frankenstein *(right). Volcanoes erupt in different ways; Tambora was the most violent kind, in which clouds of hot gas, steam and rock blast out from the volcano's crater (left).*

MOUNT PELÉE: NUCLEAR-FORCE EXPLOSION

In 1902, Mount Pelée in Martinique exploded with the force of a nuclear bomb. A super-heated cloud of gas and ash burst out of the side of the mountain, engulfing the town of St Pierre in fire. Three minutes later, the town ceased to exist. Of its 30,000 inhabitants, only a handful survived (below). The ships in the harbour sank; their passengers and crews boiled alive in the water.

When Krakatau erupted in 1883 (*right*), it was heard nearly 5,000 km (3,100 miles) away in Australia.

PETRIFIED PEOPLE AT POMPEII

The ancient Roman city of Pompeii was overshadowed by a huge volcano, Vesuvius. When this erupted in 79 AD, the whole city and its inhabitants were covered by 8 m (25 ft) of pumice and ash, which hardened around the bodies like wet cement, and created statue-like casts. These show the people at the moment of death, trying to protect themselves.

Active volcanoes almost seem to breathe... Observers of Sakura-Jima, in Japan, noticed how the volcano appeared to expand and shrink as it filled up with magma (hot, melted rock).

Historic volcanoes

"The whole mountain appeared like a body of liquid fire." *Eyewitness, Tambora, 1815*

The eruption of the volcano Tambora on an island in Indonesia (*right*) was the greatest in history, and caused worldwide destruction. Light ash fell over a 640-km (400-mile) area, followed by red-hot boulders which crushed hundreds of homes. Next, red-hot volcanic ash shot high into the atmosphere and blotted out the sun, reducing temperatures worldwide. Weather conditions changed dramatically. Cold and rain ruined harvests in Europe and, in New England, northeastern United States, snow fell in the summer, freezing laundry on the line – farmers called the year "eighteen hundred and froze to death."

Around 90,000 people died as a result of the eruption. From the start, rescue operations were ineffectual. Early explosions were mistaken for cannon fire, so the local people were not warned. The later explosions ripped the island apart, and so the governor of Java was not able to send ship-loads of rice to feed starving survivors until the volcano had blown itself out over three months later. People were left to forage the few remaining edible plants.

1 The loudest explosion ever was in 1883, when the small Indonesian island of Krakatau violently erupted.

2 As Krakatau erupted, the island collapsed, forming a 6.5-km wide (40-mile) underwater caldera (crater) and creating giant waves called *tsunamis*.

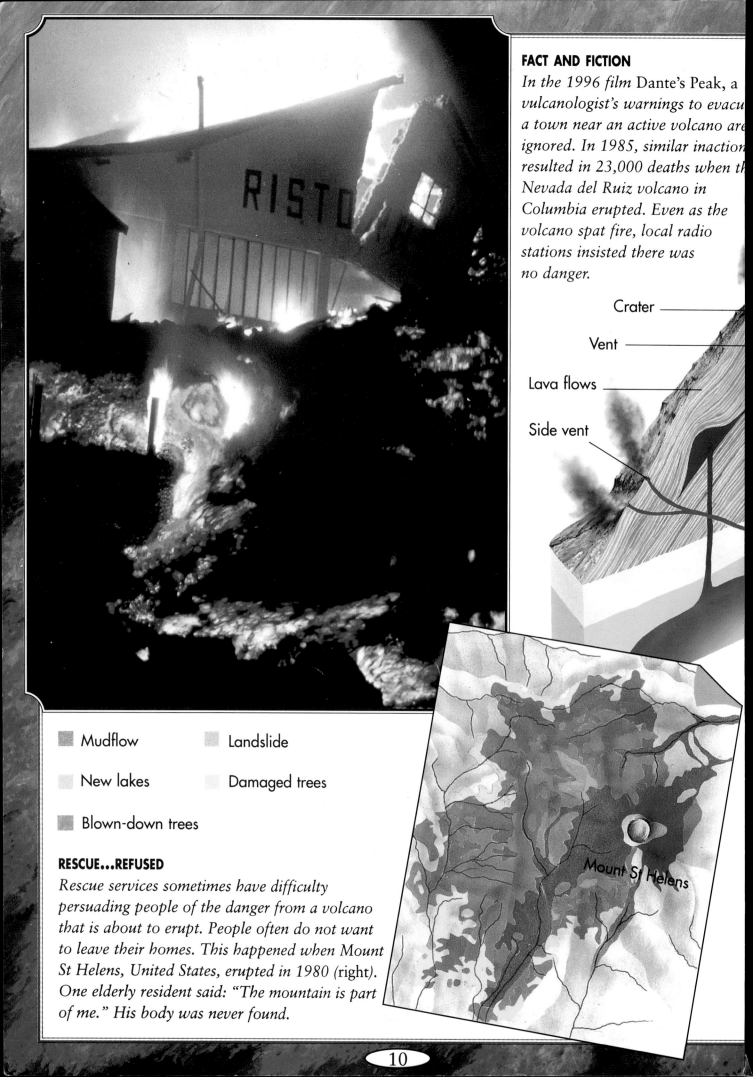

FACT AND FICTION

In the 1996 film Dante's Peak, a vulcanologist's warnings to evacu a town near an active volcano are ignored. In 1985, similar inaction resulted in 23,000 deaths when th Nevada del Ruiz volcano in Columbia erupted. Even as the volcano spat fire, local radio stations insisted there was no danger.

Crater ————

Vent ————

Lava flows ————

Side vent

Mount St Helens

- Mudflow
- New lakes
- Blown-down trees
- Landslide
- Damaged trees

RESCUE...REFUSED

Rescue services sometimes have difficulty persuading people of the danger from a volcano that is about to erupt. People often do not want to leave their homes. This happened when Mount St Helens, United States, erupted in 1980 (right). One elderly resident said: "The mountain is part of me." His body was never found.

A slice through a volcano reveals the explosive fury at its heart (*below*). Magma collects in huge chambers and, as pressure builds, is forced up through cracks in the Earth's crust. The dome is formed by successive lava flows.

— Dome

Magma chamber

Recent eruptions

"It looked like a nuclear bomb, a huge mushroom cloud over the volcano." *Eyewitness, Mount Pinatubo, 1991*

Erupting volcanoes cannot be fought: they have to be left to blow themselves out, and so it is crucial to evacuate the surrounding area.

Mount Pinatubo in the Philippines had been dormant for over 600 years.

More than 300,000 people had settled on its slopes, growing rice and raising animals on the rich volcanic soil. When it started to rumble in 1991, seismologists (people who measure Earth's vibrations), were alerted by the early-warning systems. When it began to emit smoke, the church bells were rung to sound the alarm. A small eruption followed, yet only 12,000 residents were evacuated and a nearby United States naval base closed. Two days later, a huge eruption sprayed ash over the area and disaster struck – heavy rain turned the ash to mud, causing mudflows and landslides (*above*). Without an organised evacuation plan, people panicked and fled, crushing each other on crowded roads. Two hundred people died – most of them in the mudflows rather than in the explosion itself. The area was devastated. Emergency shelters were set up in schools, churches, army camps and gymnasiums to provide food, shelter, first-aid and clothes for the thousands of refugees.

LIVING IN THE SHADOW OF A VOLCANO

Despite the ever-present threat of eruptions, people are reluctant to move away from their homes. Instead, they make the most of what they have. The mineral-rich volcanic soil (ash), is ideal for farming and many towns use their volcanoes as a source of tourist income, such as this café beside Mount Pinatubo (left).

In 1872, a group of tourists were so engrossed in the spectacle of Mount Etna's bubbling crater that they were engulfed by a stream of red-hot lava.

VOLCANO Special
LAVA FLOWS in FIELDS AVE.
(We Will Buy You A Drink!)
½ PRICE 2 for 1
DURING POISON GAS
VOLCANIC ASHES & ROCKS
HAPPY HOUR ▷ 2 A.M. 2 P.M.

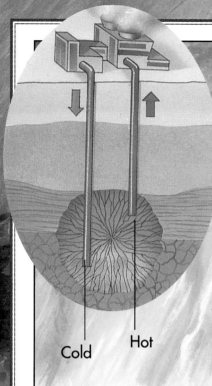

POWER FROM THE GROUND

Hot rocks below the Earth's surface can be used to provide an endless source of energy. Geothermal power stations use steam from heated water to turn turbines which produce electricity. Water is pumped into the ground at sites where there are hot rocks within a few kilometres of the surface. The heated water is then piped back to the surface as steam.

Cold   Hot

MONITORING BY LASER

When magma rises in a volcano, the slopes may bulge, indicating that it may erupt. Lasers are often trained on a volcano's sides to detect this movement, which registers as a change in length of the beam.

Volcanoes in the future

"When you are really close to the action you have no time to be afraid..."   *Maurice Krafft, 1991*

They may look dramatic on television or in photographs, but most people would not choose to be nearby when a volcano blows. Yet for vulcanologists Maurice and Katia Krafft, news of an eruption would send them racing for the first plane to the stricken region. This husband and wife team was passionate about their work, and they observed many explosions to improve scientists' understanding of why and when volcanoes erupt. Tragically, the Kraffts were killed by the eruption of Mount Unzen, in Japan, in 1991. Whilst some vulcanologists operate from the safety of laboratories, many risk their lives to work on the volcano itself (*above*).

Every day, at least one volcano erupts somewhere in the world. Vulcanologists look for early-warning signs such as earth tremors and escaping gases, as even a day's warning can allow enough time to evacuate the area.

The people of Montserrat, in the West Indies, live in the shadow of a volcano on their island which erupts periodically – the 1997 eruptions ruined the livelihood of many islanders. Montserrat's future is uncertain. Its volcano may continue to erupt on a small-scale or could explode violently, destroying the island.

On a global scale, scientists predict that the 21st century will be one of the most explosive on record. Rising sea levels, caused by global warming, are likely to trigger volcanic activity, creating new volcanoes and activating existing ones.

GHOST TOWN

The volcanic eruptions on Montserrat in 1997 wreaked havoc. By December, just 4,000 islanders (fewer than half) were left on the island and the capital, Plymouth, was virtually wiped off the map (below).

Red-hot rivers of lava can wipe out towns. Here, dynamite is being used to divert a flow from Mount Etna, Italy, into an inactive crater (*above*).

The village of Zafferana is under threat from lava from Etna (*below*).

Those people on Montserrat who lost their homes have had to move to nearby islands or live in temporary shelters.

ETNA ERUPTS... AND ERUPTS...

In 1979, tourists on the Mediterranean island of Sicily were horrified to see a crater open up at their feet! The locals, however, just sighed: they're used to it. Mount Etna on Sicily has been erupting on and off for at least the last 2,500 years, and regularly destroys villages and farmland. The last major eruption took place in 1992. Officials have learned to limit the damage by diverting the lava flow. Using a crane (or bulldozers), they block the lava's route by creating a high wall of rock and earth (right).

ENDANGERING THE RESCUERS

In the 19th century, horse-drawn fire engines could be highly dangerous: fire-fighters clung on to the sides as the vehicles travelled at high speed, and some were killed when they fell off. Many fire-fighters were volunteers who had full-time jobs nearby, and therefore could get to the fire engine quickly. In London, they wore blue uniforms and huge, heavy, gleaming brass helmets.

TEAMWORK

Fighting fires in a city requires teamwork. Where buildings lie so close together, flames can spread quickly. Each team has a special task, such as searching for trapped people or connecting hoses to water hydrants in the road. The water is directed at the centre of the blaze to dampen as much flammable material as possible.

FIRE ENGINES PAST AND PRESENT

The harnessing of steam power in the 19th century brought fire-fighting into the modern age. Vehicles such as the Sutherland steam fire engine (above right) were pulled by teams of horses and could pump a stream of water almost 30 m (100 ft). Before bells were introduced in 1903, one of the fire-fighters had the job of shouting "hi-hi" to warn people to get out of the way. Modern fire engines carry long ladders, breathing apparatus and equipment to deal with almost any situation (left).

THE RIGHT CLOTHES FOR THE JOB

To be effective at fighting fires, modern fire-fighters must be specially trained, have the proper transport and equipment, and be well protected (right). They wear flame-resistant clothes and carry special breathing apparatus so that they will not be suffocated by the deadly smoke that a fire produces.

Generator

Heavy-duty cutter

Modern aerial tillers have highly manoeuvrable ladders which extend to 30 m (100 ft).

eathing apparatus

Fire-fighters

"Fire-fighters are modern heroes. They risk their lives to save others." *Survivor, house fire, 1997*

Why do people become fire-fighters? Do fire-fighters enter a building where a blazing inferno rages just because it is their job? When asked, most of them describe the sense of being part of a close team, which is willing to accept the professional and personal challenge of fighting fire, along with the desire to help those in distress.

Before organised fire-fighting forces were set up in the 19th century, blazes were fought by volunteers, assisted by anyone available to help. The most vital piece of fire-fighting equipment was the bucket, passed from hand to hand to deliver water to the fire. To tackle a city-wide blaze, buildings were blown up or pulled down using long hooks on ropes, to create firebreaks (areas containing nothing that could burn).

Over time, fire-fighting efficiency improved; first with the introduction of steam-power (*left*) – used to pump water, then after 1900, through the internal-combustion engine. Modern fire-fighters, such as 'les pompiers' in France, train as paramedics and attend all types of emergency.

Electrical fires

Lightning *does* strike in the same place twice: the Empire State Building is struck about 25 times a year.

A single lightning bolt discharges about 100 million volts of electricity – a force great enough to blow up buildings, start fires and kill people. At any one time, there are about 1,800 thunderstorms raging through the sky and, on average, 100 people a year are killed by lightning in the United States alone. One of the unluckiest victims was US park ranger, Roy Sullivan – he was hit by lightning a record seven times. His eyebrows were burnt off, his hair was set alight, his ankle was damaged and his shoulder, chest and stomach were all burnt. He eventually died in 1983 – of causes unrelated to lightning.

In a storm, it is dangerous to be near tall objects, such as trees, hill tops, telegraph poles, and ships (*left*), as lightning will strike the highest point on a landscape.

Electricity in the home can also be lethal. About one third of all household fires are caused by faulty or carelessly-used electrical appliances, such as kettles and toasters. More fires start in this way than by any other cause, including accidents when cooking.

FIRES ON BOATS

Most ports have fire-fighting tugboats (below) to fight fires which break out on ships. Boat fires are often sparked off by faults in the electrical circuitry. Special extinguishers must be used, as water has no effect on electrical fires and creates the added risk of electrocution for the fire-fighters. Lifeboats are also equipped to fight fires.

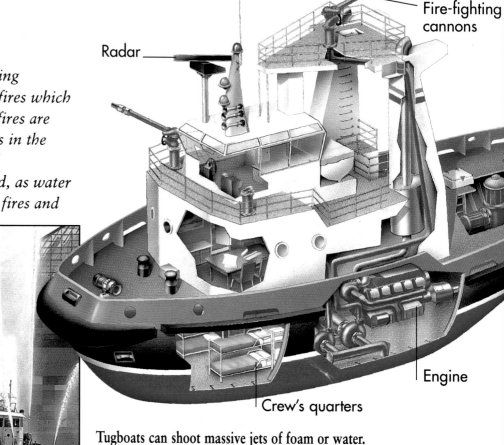

Radar

Fire-fighting cannons

Engine

Crew's quarters

Tugboats can shoot massive jets of foam or water.

PLAYING WITH FIRE

In 1752, the American scientist Benjamin Franklin proved that lightning is electricity (below). He flew a kite, with a key tied to one end, during a thunderstorm. Franklin was lucky not to have been electrocuted when sparks came down the wet string and struck the key.

It took just 30 seconds for the *Hindenburg* to crash in flames.

HINDENBURG DISASTER

On 6 May, 1937, over 100 passengers were onboard the airship Hindenburg – *then the modern way to cross the Atlantic – when a ball of fire, possibly sparked by lightning or a build up of static electricity on the outside, burst through its cover. The hydrogen gas used to lift the airship was ablaze in seconds and passengers watched in horror as flames licked the windows of their luxury accommodation. Some jumped to safety, but 36 died in the tragedy.*

LIGHTNING-STRUCK AEROPLANES

Aircraft are vulnerable to lightning strikes. Although their fuselage is designed to conduct lightning around it, accidents still happen (left). In 1974, lightning knocked the nose cone off an American aeroplane, forcing it to make an emergency landing.

FIGHTING ELECTRICAL FIRES

Fire extinguishers for use on electrical fires (right) shoot out a 'snow' of solid carbon dioxide. This excludes oxygen from the fire and lowers the temperature, preventing further burning from taking place.

City fires

● Destruction of the first day

● Destruction of the second day

● Destruction of the third day

"All the sky were of a fiery aspect, like the top of a burning oven..." *John Evelyn, diarist, on the Fire of London, 1666*

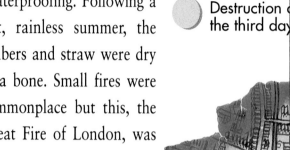

In Pudding Lane, London, at two o'clock in the morning of Sunday 2 September, 1666, a baker and his family were awakened by smoke and flames coming from their bakery. They managed to escape by clambering over the roofs of their neighbours' houses, but the fire spread quickly from house to house. Soon, whole streets were alight – the flames fanned by strong winds. London, like most large towns of the time (including Nuremburg in Germany, *above*), was full of wooden houses packed tightly together. Their roofs were thatched with straw and coated with pitch (a highly flammable substance) for waterproofing. Following a hot, rainless summer, the timbers and straw were dry as a bone. Small fires were commonplace but this, the Great Fire of London, was something else. There were no official fire-fighting forces at this time so disorganised bands of ordinary people were left to pass buckets of water to the flames. Houses were blown up to stop the fire spreading, filling the air with the sound and smell of gunpowder. Nothing could stop the raging blaze until, after four days, the wind dropped and it began to die down.

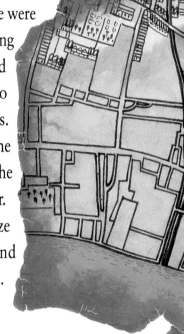

FIGHTING FIRES WITH WATER PISTOLS

The first known fire engines were invented by the ancient Romans. They were like large buckets on wheels (below), with two hand-operated pumps on either side which produced a jet of water.

Similar engines were still being used during the Great Fire of London in 1666. The hoses were not powerful enough to shoot water to the tops of buildings. Hand-held pumps, which worked like large syringes, or water pistols, were also used – but were equally ineffectual.

ROME BURNS

The mad Roman Emperor Nero ordered the burning of Rome in 64 AD (below), so that he could expand his palace. Gangs of thugs attacked those who tried to put out the flames, which burned for six days.

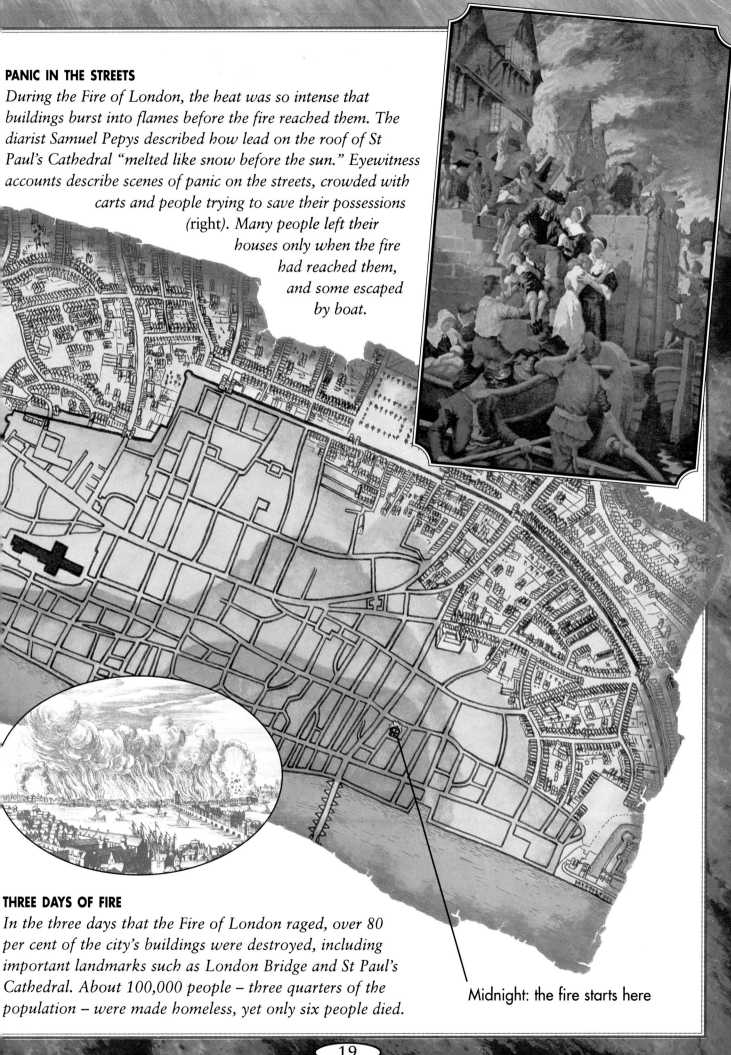

PANIC IN THE STREETS

During the Fire of London, the heat was so intense that buildings burst into flames before the fire reached them. The diarist Samuel Pepys described how lead on the roof of St Paul's Cathedral "melted like snow before the sun." Eyewitness accounts describe scenes of panic on the streets, crowded with carts and people trying to save their possessions (right). Many people left their houses only when the fire had reached them, and some escaped by boat.

THREE DAYS OF FIRE

In the three days that the Fire of London raged, over 80 per cent of the city's buildings were destroyed, including important landmarks such as London Bridge and St Paul's Cathedral. About 100,000 people – three quarters of the population – were made homeless, yet only six people died.

Midnight: the fire starts here

19

BURNING OF MOSCOW

In 1812, more than 100,000 people in Moscow, Russia, were made homeless when their city was torched by Cossacks (the Tsar's soldiers) when the army of the invading French general, Napoleon, entered the city. Cossack policy was to set fire to houses as they were retreating, so that the enemy could not use them. The fire spread quickly, engulfing the wooden buildings.

Most of Moscow was destroyed by fires in 1812.

FIREBOMBING OF DRESDEN

For five days in February 1943, 1,500 bombers attacked Dresden, reducing it to a smoking ruin; they even returned to bomb the fire-fighters. The fire storm caused the deaths of more than 130,000 civilians. Fire-fighters had to wait for the flames to burn themselves out. The people of Dresden worked together to rebuild their city after the war; here, a human chain is formed to carry bricks.

Wartime fires

"The policy is obliteration, openly acknowledged."
The Bishop of Chichester, Britain, condemning fire storms, 1944

For 43 minutes during World War II, the German city of Hamburg was bombarded with incendiary bombs dropped by allied planes. The whole city was set ablaze, killing 40,000 people, turning a further million into refugees, and making fire-fighting impossible. Many people found it difficult to breathe. Burning debris scattered over a wide area, causing further fires and even more heat. The Hamburg fire department had never seen anything like it. They called it a 'Feuersturm', or fire storm. A fire storm is created when intensive bombing in a built-up area, such as a

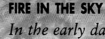

city, creates extremely high temperatures. Great heat within a confined space causes hot air to rise quickly, sucking in vast amounts of air from every direction. The fires quickly unite into one massive inferno, creating gale force winds and temperatures of over 800°C (1500°F). As intended, the bombing of Hamburg created a climate of fear in every German city: people said "what happened to Hamburg yesterday can happen to us tomorrow."

People in Beirut, the capital of Lebanon, in the Middle East, have lived in fear since the mid-1970s, when war broke out between Christian and Muslim groups. Fires were started in many areas (*above*), causing extensive damage throughout the city.

Israel launches its *Patriot* missiles to shoot down Iraqi *Scud* missiles in February 1991.

FIRE IN THE SKY

In the early days of the Gulf War (1990-91), Iraq attacked Tel Aviv, the capital of Israel, with Scud *missiles. The Israelis fought back with* Patriot *missiles which are sophisticated rockets controlled by radar, and can detect approaching* Scuds *from about 112 km (70 miles) away. They blow up the* Scuds *in mid-air creating huge fires in the sky (left). Big chunks of both missiles often fall to the ground. It is thought that the amount of damage and number of casualties in Israel increased once* Patriots *were deployed there: sometimes the* Patriots *only damaged* Scuds *or pushed them off course.*

Building fires

"I saw people run through a barrier of fire with their hair and clothing in flames." *Janitor, Joelma Building, 1974*

On the morning of 1 February, 1974, 650 people were working in the 25-storey San Joelma building in São Paulo, Brazil, when a fire broke out on the 11th floor. It spread quickly, fuelled by the flammable plastic furniture. The building had virtually no fire escapes and the fire brigade's ladders only reached halfway up the building. Those trapped on the upper floors were helpless. Many desperate people clung screaming to the window ledges – some jumped rather than wait for the flames to devour them or to be overcome by smoke (a common cause of death in fires). The fire services tried shooting ropes across from a nearby building, and one brave fire-fighter rescued 18 people in this way. A further 100 were evacuated from the roof by helicopters. More than 200 people died in the 700°C (1300°F) inferno, with a further 250 people seriously injured or burned.

Blazing buildings are a terrifying sight (*left*) although, since the Joelma tragedy, many buildings have been made safer by the use of smoke detectors, sprinkler systems and fire doors.

CASTLE IN FLAMES

In 1992, Windsor Castle, a home of the British royal family, was ravaged by a blaze which took 15 hours and two million gallons of water to put out (below). Priceless works of art were hurled to safety from the balconies.

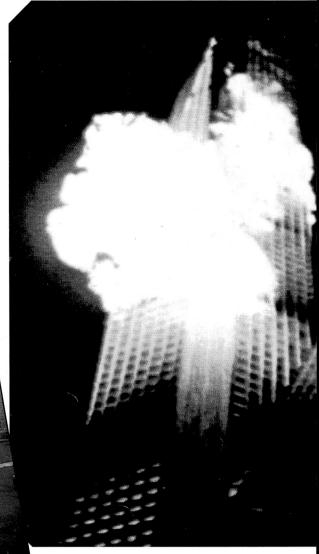

Fire engulfs the top floors of the office block in the 1974 film *The Towering Inferno* (*above*).

FIRE EXTINGUISHERS

Depending on the solution being forced out on to the fire, extinguishers use different firing methods: either pressurised carbon dioxide (CO_2) gas (1 and 3) or pressure caused by a violent reaction between sulphuric acid and sodium bicarbonate (2).

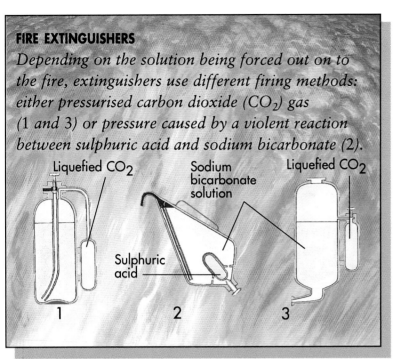

Liquefied CO_2

Sodium bicarbonate solution

Liquefied CO_2

Sulphuric acid

1   2   3

Remote-controlled robots – the new first line of defence against fires?

ROBOT HELPERS

Where human fire-fighters dare not venture, the robot steps in. This remote-controlled machine, with its powerful water hose, is used to reach fires in very small places or in places too dangerous for people to go. Some robotic fire-fighting machines can walk up the outsides of buildings to reach blazes on upper floors quickly. Advanced robots are currently being developed that will be able to move by sensing their surroundings.

INFERNO

The Joelma office block tragedy was the inspiration for the 1974 film, The Towering Inferno (left). In the film, people are trapped on the floors above a fire in the tallest skyscraper in town, making rescue almost impossible. The fire is extinguished by blowing up the water supply room to flood the building. The film vividly brought to life the terror of fires in buildings.

Fire-fighters take the heat in *The Towering Inferno* (*above*).

A fire-fighter burns an area of forest scrub to provide a barren area that breaks the advance of a serious forest fire.

TACKLING LARGE-SCALE FIRES

Water bombers (below) are aeroplanes that carry large tanks of water which can be released over a wide area of burning woodland. It takes seconds for the tank to be emptied, after which the crew takes the plane back to the airfield to be refilled. Some types of water bomber can fly over lakes or seas to scoop up extra water.

The biggest risk of forest fires occurs following a dry spell when the wood and vegetation are tinder dry. The fires start in a number of ways: human carelessness accounts for many, although they can also be caused by lightning or by the sun's rays magnified through discarded glass.

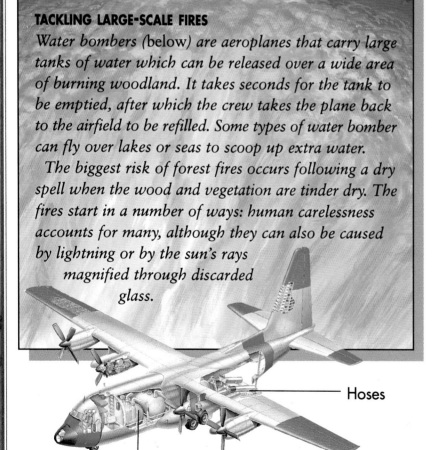

Hoses

Water tanks

OUT OF CONTROL

In 1997, fires raged through forests in Indonesia, encouraged by drought thought to result from a weather condition called El Niño. The whole area was clouded in thick, choking smog. The southern hemisphere was further plagued by a series of fires surrounding the city of Sydney, in Australia. Drought, heat and high winds created the worst bush fire conditions in 30 years. Temperatures soared as fire-fighters struggled to contain the lightning-sparked blazes.

Forest fires

"It came in great sheeted flames from heaven."
A survivor describing the Lake Michigan fire, 1871

Forest fires are both terrifying and lethal. Giant flames leap from tree to tree, beneath huge clouds of smoke (*right*).

They move erratically, leap-frogging some areas to ignite the trees beyond and then returning to destroy the small islands they missed. Animals flee ahead of the pursuing wall of flames; people try to escape the heat by hiding in water tanks or wells, or by sheltering under wet blankets.

One of the world's worst forest fires was

in America in 1871, when a wall of flame swept rapidly along the shores of Lake Michigan, destroying over a million acres of forest and killing more than 1,000 people. Survivors describe a whirlwind of flames that rose above the treetops. Some people were killed by breathing in the super-heated air.

Fighting forest fires requires a two-pronged attack. First, specialist crews fly over the blaze in water bombers. Then, once the blaze is under control, regular fire-fighters attend the scene. Hundreds of extras from the army or civilian populations may be called in as reinforcements.

A helicopter hovers above a forest fire, ready to drop water from its bucket (*above*).

THE AFTERMATH
Fire-fighters move in to beat out a forest fire (above). These fires can be extremely difficult to deal with because of the speed at which they move and the enormous temperatures that are reached. In Australia, the heat of a bush fire twisted huge steel girders and machinery as if they were toys.

Oil and chemical fires

"It was as though the platform had been blown up by an atomic bomb." *Survivor, Piper Alpha, 1988*

In July 1988, 226 workers were aboard the Piper Alpha oil-rig in the North Sea – 62 of them working the night-shift, others watching a film in the onboard cinema. Suddenly they heard an explosion from the gas-processing area and, as the men rushed for their survival suits, the lights on the rig went out. As fire spread, the radio operator screamed: "The radio room is on fire; we've got to get out of here." To escape, the men had to leap 61 m (200 ft) into a sea roaring with blazing oil. The intense heat from the rig hampered rescue operations, and bubbles of gas burst up from the pipes below, igniting as they reached the surface. High-speed rescue dinghies dodged the flames to rescue survivors.

Chemical fires, including gas- and oil-related blazes and those at chemical and industrial plants, are some of the hardest to tackle. Substances which cause the fire are often unstable and can be explosive, creating added risks for fire-fighters (*left*). Further danger is caused by toxic fumes which can spread in billowing clouds over a wide area: nuclear accidents pose the threat of radioactive contamination.

EMERGENCY SUPPORT VEHICLES

For months at a time, these huge floating platforms are home to more than 90 people (right). Emergency Support Vehicles (ESVs) patrol the open sea, many kilometres from land, ready to attend to fires or accidents at oil-rigs. They provide a mobile base for helicopters, rescue boats and diving teams. Up to 17 water guns are positioned around the vessel, which can pump water to a distance of 180 m (590 ft). Foam stored in the corner columns is used to smother burning oil.

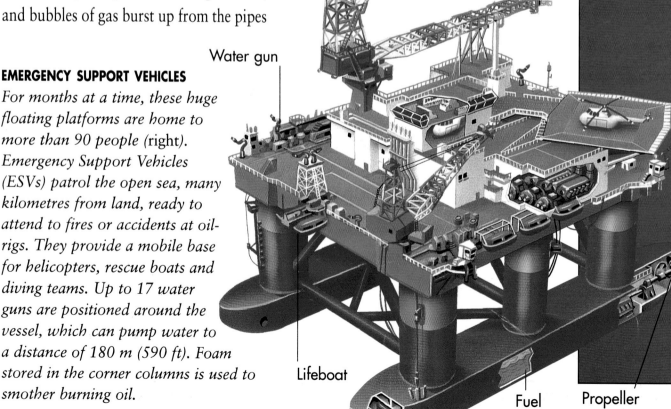

Water gun

Lifeboat

Fuel

Propeller

BURNING OIL WELLS

This oil-well in the Middle Eastern country of Iran has caught fire and experts are trying to put it out. During the Gulf War of 1990-91, in an act of environmental terrorism, the defeated Iraqi army set fire to Kuwaiti oil-wells as they retreated from their occupation of the country. The blazes took months to extinguish.

THE BHOPAL DISASTER

In 1984, an explosion at a pesticide factory near Bhopal, India, released a thick cloud of gas containing toxic chemicals over the city. Hundreds of people choked to death in their sleep. At least 50,000 were seriously injured and will have damaged lungs or eyesight for the rest of their lives (below).

PIPER ALPHA DISASTER

The Emergency Support Vehicle (ESV) Tharos *directs its powerful fire-fighting guns at the Piper Alpha oil-rig, which is almost obscured by smoke. Boats were launched from the ESV to pick up the survivors from the water; 167 men died in the disaster.*

The fire-stricken Piper Alpha tilts as its legs give way.

Freak fires

"The flames burst outwards, as if they originated within her body." *Witness of spontaneous combustion*

Some kinds of 'fire' are not really fire at all. Saint Elmo's fire, for example, is a kind of blue glow sometimes seen around ships' masts or high-altitude aeroplanes. It is not fire, but static electricity, which is produced in the air during storms.

Another odd phenomenon is marsh light (sometimes called Will o' the Wisp), which appears as a pale flame flickering in the air above bogs and marshes. It is caused by rotting vegetation which gives off smoky gases that burn easily.

Some deep-sea fishes, like the anglerfish (*above*), carry their own glowing light, called 'bioluminescence': the light is caused by chemical reactions in the skin.

Perhaps the oddest incidence of fire is 'spontaneous human combustion' – a phenomena in which the victim's body is reduced to a pile of oily ashes, whilst leaving the surrounding area barely charred. Despite the many well-documented cases over the last 300 years, investigators still can't agree whether the flames have an external cause, such as a nearby fire, or whether they truly come from within.

GLOW-IN-THE-DARK BUGS

There is something magical about the sight of fireflies silently floating in the air, flashing yellow light. Fireflies are actually night-flying beetles which glow in the dark due to an internal chemical reaction. They use the light they produce to help them see in the dark and for signalling and courtship. Flightless fireflies, called glow-worms, were once used as reading lamps!

BALL LIGHTNING

Some people claim to have seen a form of lightning called "ball lightning" (above). It is a glowing, fiery ball that floats for a short while before disappearing.

HE LEFT HIS BOOTS!

The British author Charles Dickens (1812-70) believed in spontaneous human combustion, and wrote it into one of his novels, Bleak House. *The charred corpse of Krook is found in an otherwise intact room – but nothing else has burnt. From his letters, we know that Dickens based this account on reports of an actual case of human combustion.*

Kirlian photography is a special technique that captures the aura, or halo, apparently given off by people. It is said to come from electric energy and changes according to mood. High frequency electro-photography was pioneered by a Russian electrician called Semyon Kirlian in 1939.

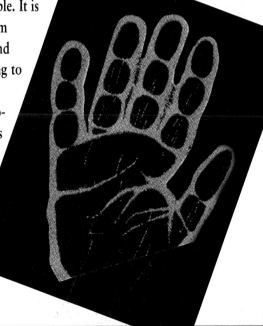

Some people are reported to be able to start fires by the power of their minds. The 1976 horror film *Carrie* tells the story of a young woman with these powers.

Emergency first-aid

Here is some practical advice for emergencies involving fire.

If a fire breaks out in your house:

- Close all the doors and get out of the building as quickly as possible.
- Do not stop to pick up any belongings.
- If you get trapped, block gaps under doors where fire or smoke could get in.
- If smoke is coming into the room, crawl on the floor and open a window to call for help.
- If you need to jump, drop bedding onto the ground first.

Different types of burn require specific treatment:

- **Thermal (fire, heat, steam, hot liquids or hot objects):** Wet with cold water or smother the burn. Remove smouldering clothing.
- **Chemical (acids and caustic material):** Rinse the burn with lots of water for at least 20 minutes.
- **Electrical (AC current, DC current, lightning):** DO NOT TOUCH the victim until contact with the current has been broken. Switch off the current if possible, or stand on a dry object and push the victim away from the source using a dry broomstick. The victim may need resuscitating by a trained first-aider.
- **Hot tar, grease or wax:** Cool with water, but do not try to remove substance from the burn.

Remember:

- Get the victim to hospital as soon as possible.
- Do not put anything other than water on a burn.
- NEVER put ice on a burn.
- Carefully remove clothing or jewellery that could become too tight should the area swell.
- Do not remove any clothing that is stuck to the burn.

Glossary

Active A term used to describe a volcano that may erupt at any time.

Ash Tiny fragments of rock and lava blown out of a volcano during an eruption.

Bioluminescence The ability of some animals and plants to give off light. Examples include fireflies and some deep-sea fishes. The light is produced by chemical reactions in the body or by the action of microscopic bacteria.

Carbon dioxide A gas produced by fires.

Crust The solid, outer layer of the Earth. Underneath the crust, temperatures are so high that rocks melt into a fiery liquid called magma.

Dormant A volcano that has not erupted for a long time but may still be active in the future.

Electricity A form of energy produced by the movement of charged atomic particles (electrons and protons).

Element Basic building block of everything on Earth. There once thought to be just four elements: air, earth, fire and water.

Erupt To throw out hot rocks, gases and other material through a hole in the Earth's surface.

Extinct A volcano which has not erupted for thousands of years and which experts do not think will erupt again.

Firebreak A specially prepared open space, containing little or nothing to burn and designed to stop the spread of a fire.

Fire storm An intense fire (caused by incendiary bombing) that causes violent winds to be sucked towards its centre.

Foam A combination of water and a foaming agent used to extinguish electrical and chemical fires.

Geothermal energy Energy that comes from heat inside the Earth.

Hotspot A crack in the Earth's crust below the ocean floor through which magma escapes to form volcanoes.

Incendiary bomb A bomb that contains explosives which spread fire. Incendiary bombs usually contain the chemical phosphorus, which ignites on contact with air.

Inferno A large, destructive fire; the word actually refers to any place or area that resembles hell.

Lava Magma which pours out of volcanoes or cracks in the Earth's crust.

Magma Red-hot, molten rock found inside the Earth, below the crust.

Oil-rig A platform used for drilling and extracting oil. Off-shore oil-rigs float on the water's surface and are anchored to the sea bed.

Pesticide Chemical used to treat crops and protect them from pests, such as insects, fungi, bacteria and weeds.

'Ring of Fire' The name given to the area along the edge of the Pacific Ocean where many of the world's earthquakes and volcanoes occur.

Seismologist A scientist who studies ground movements.

Tsunami A huge wave caused by movement of the seabed following an earthquake or the eruption of an underwater volcano.

Vulcanologist Scientist who studies volcanoes.

Index